"Human dignity—that of the convicted as well as our own—is best served by not resorting to this extreme and unnecessary punishment. As *Death Penalty and Discipleship: A Faith Formation Guide* makes clear: Modern society has the means to protect itself without the death penalty."

— Archbishop Thomas Wenski
Archdiocese of Miami

"David McCarthy's *Death Penalty and Discipleship* is an accessible, practical resource that is perfectly designed for use in study groups, parishes and classrooms. Yet while engaging and accessible with its video clips reference and reflection questions, it is written by one of the American Church's most important theologians. This rich book will reward users, and is a perfect example of placing theological expertise at the service of the people of God."

— William C. Mattison III
The Catholic University of America

"This text will serve as an invaluable resource for those seeking to engage in formation of conscience, both personally and communally, around the practice of capital punishment. Small faith communities, parishes, and adult faith formation programs will find it accessible, thoughtful, and well grounded in Scripture and the wisdom of ecclesial tradition."

— Margaret Pfeil
The University of Notre Dame

Death Penalty and Discipleship

A Faith Formation Guide

David Matzko McCarthy

LITURGICAL PRESS

Collegeville, Minnesota

www.litpress.org

1	2	3	4	5	6	7	8	9

Library of Congress Cataloging-in-Publication Data

McCarthy, David Matzko.
   Death penalty and discipleship : a faith formation guide / by David Matzko McCarthy.
      pages cm
    ISBN 978-0-8146-4809-4 — ISBN 978-0-8146-4834-6 (ebook)
     1. Capital punishment—Religious aspects—Christianity.
  2. Capital punishment—Religious aspects—Catholic Church.
  3. Catholic Church—Doctrines.   I. Title.

   HV8698.M355   2015
   261.8'3366—dc23

                                         2014048522

Contents

Preface

This book comes to you through the good work of the Catholic Mobilizing Network (www.catholicsmobilizing.org). The Catholic Mobilizing Network (CMN) is founded on the church's unconditional call to be pro-life and to live in response to God's redemption and reconciliation in Jesus Christ. Established in 2008, the CMN takes up the challenge of the US bishops to end the use of the death penalty and to build a culture of life.[1]

In recent years, the CMN's work to end the death penalty has developed through a promotion of restorative justice. A concern for restorative justice also highlights the teaching of the church. In the words of the US bishops:

> Punishment alone cannot address complex social problems in communities, or effectively help end cycles of crime and violence. A restorative justice approach is more comprehensive and addresses the needs of victims, the community and those responsible for causing harm through healing, prevention, education, rehabilitation and community support.[2]

The church's call to end the death penalty and promotion of restorative justice are two sides of the same coin.

The Death Penalty and Discipleship provides a study of the death penalty in terms of God's presence and self-giving in Jesus Christ and the implications of God's work for how we view the death penalty. Along the way, we will examine Scripture, especially difficult passages like the well-known requirement to punish another by taking "an eye for an eye" (Lev 24:19-20). We will also consider the *Catechism of the Catholic Church* and its teachings on punishment as well as capital punishment.

We will ponder the difficult question, Would you want the death penalty if a son or daughter, mother or father, husband or wife were murdered? How we answer this question goes to the heart of what St. John Paul II has called the "new evangelization." Consider the response of the archbishop of Kansas City, Kansas, Joseph F. Naumann, whose father was murdered in 1948, a few months before Joseph was born: "Our refusal to resort to the death penalty is not because we fail to appreciate the horror of the crime committed, but because we refuse to imitate violent criminals."[3] On the contrary, the new evangelization is a renewed and expansive call to imitate our Lord in all of life—for our transformation and for the transformation of the world. The church's call for the end of the death penalty is a call to the culture of life.

My own hope for you, as you make your way through the book, is that you are renewed in your faith. For me, this book is not so much about the death penalty, but about our restoration in God's love and the joy of the Christian life.

June 29
Solemnity of Saints Peter and Paul
David M. McCarthy

1

God Is the Giver of Life

The first topic in our study of capital punishment is God's self-giving and his gifts of reconciliation and redemption. After all, God's goodness is the beginning of everything. Specifically in relationship to the death penalty, we Christians should bring to light our convictions that God is the giver of life. The church is called to be pro-life. The church's pro-life efforts are an essential part of its mission and evangelization of the world, and that mission includes the church's stance against the death penalty. God loves the world and gives himself to the world, and we are called to share God's justice, love, and mercy with others.

Our call to be just, loving, and merciful is emphasized by Pope Francis in his apostolic exhortation on the proclamation of the Gospel (*Evangelii Gaudium*). Francis emphasizes God's free grace and our loving response:

> The Church which "goes forth" is a community of missionary disciples . . . An evangelizing community knows that the Lord has taken the initiative, he has loved us first (cf. *1 Jn* 4:19), and therefore we can move forward, boldly take the initiative, go out to others, seek those who have fallen away,

stand at the crossroads and welcome the outcast. Such a community has an endless desire to show mercy, the fruit of its own experience of the power of the Father's infinite mercy.[1]

Papal Message Reaffirms Call to Abolish Death Penalty

In June 2013, Pope Francis sent a message to participants of a World Congress Against the Death Penalty held in Madrid.

His message placed the abolition of the death penalty alongside other pro-life issues.

"Today, more than ever, it is urgent that we remember and affirm the need for universal recognition and respect for the inalienable dignity of human life, in its immeasurable value."

(www.ncregister.com/daily-news/papal-message-reaffirms-call-to
-abolish-death-penalty/)

Following Pope Francis's exhortation to the church, this chapter provides a short review of salvation history and the loving mercy of God. The center point and fulfillment of salvation history is God's self-giving. The center point is the incarnation of God in Jesus Christ, his death on the cross, and his resurrection to new life. The reality of God's self-giving love and mercy is the perspective from which we will consider the issue of capital punishment.

The Choice: Jesus or Barabbas

"If Jesus had lived and died in contemporary times, the basic Christian symbol would not be a cross but an electric chair. We would have an electric chair on the altar." This is a provocative claim. It was repeated often by a classmate of mine in seminary. Christopher liked to make people think. He was confrontational and argumentative. (And it makes perfect sense that he is now a successful lawyer.) As I recall, Chris was not making a point about capital punishment. As a provocateur, he was just trying to shake us up a bit. As annoying as he often was, he was right. I did need some shaking up. I had become too settled and too accustomed to the crucifix as a comfort to me. I often did forget that the cross represents Jesus' suffering, not only his agonizing death of crucifixion, but also the dread of being forsaken by his people and his friends. His people handed him over to the Romans. His closest confidants, like Peter, abandoned him. Yet, at the very moment that we turn away from God, he gives himself to us.

The crucifixion of Jesus was a traumatic event. These days, the pain of the event is never clearer to me than on Palm/Passion Sunday when the passion story is read. You might recall that the whole congregation takes the part of the crowd that gathers after Jesus' trial. The people are given an option by Pontius Pilate. He offers to release Jesus, but we demand Barabbas. When Pilate asks us what we want him to do with Jesus, we say, "Crucify him." Saying those words is unsettling for me. When I was younger, I believed that Jesus' enemies had gone through the crowd and convinced the people to be against Jesus. I imagined that most people had been tricked somehow. Since then I have learned that the common people had their own reasons to abandon Jesus. To his contemporaries, Jesus appeared to have failed in his mission to bring the kingdom of God.

Jesus is God's self-giving. The choice for Barabbas represents the ways of the world. Faith in Jesus is trust in the ways of God. Barabbas was imprisoned as an insurrectionist. He called for violent rebellion against Rome. Jesus was arrested and brought before Pilate on a similar charge. But, unlike Barabbas, Jesus did not call for insurrection against Rome. He did not call for rebellion. Because he was not initiating armed conflict, it seemed that he was not going to deliver on the promised kingdom of God. Maybe the people thought that Barabbas would. It seemed that Jesus' decisive moment had come and gone without the liberation that the Jews were hoping for. He had entered Jerusalem as Messiah and King, and then he went down without a fight. Without a fight, he was arrested by Jewish authorities and sent to

Pilate as a broken man. At least, that is how it must have seemed. Jesus was executed by Rome. Rome was the great empire of the world and the oppressor of the Jewish people. His execution at the hands of the Romans appeared to be evidence that Jesus was not the redeemer of Israel.

This view—that Jesus' mission had come to a bitter end—was the topic of conversation between two followers of Jesus on the road to Emmaus. They traveled to Emmaus shortly after Jesus' crucifixion, and they met with a fellow traveler (whom they didn't recognize as Jesus). They told him about their disappointment and despair (Luke 24:20-21). Jesus' execution on the cross was the opposite of what Jesus' disciples and admirers expected. Consider Peter's shock and annoyance when Jesus taught his disciples about his coming death (Mark 8:27-33). In response to the question "Who do people say that I am?," Peter declared, "You are the Messiah." Jesus gave a surprising response to Peter's answer. He said that he would suffer and be killed. Peter rebuked him. After all, Peter had just named Jesus as the Messiah, and the Messiah was supposed to rule over Jerusalem, not die there. But Jesus turned the rebuke onto Peter: "Get behind me, Satan. You are thinking not as God does, but as human beings do."

John Paul II's Devotion to Divine Mercy

In the second year of his pontificate, John Paul II issued an encyclical on divine and human mercy, *Dives in Misericordia.*

In the encyclical, he points to Christ's mission of mercy, which "becomes the program of His people, the program of the Church" (8).

"Jesus Christ taught that man not only receives and experiences the mercy of God, but that he is also called 'to practice mercy' towards others: 'Blessed are the merciful, for they shall obtain mercy'" (Matt 5:7) (14).

God's ways are not our ways. God's path is not our usual way of doing things; it is a way of surprising love and boundless mercy. God's way is the way of our salvation. When Peter declared that Jesus was the Messiah, he could not imagine how Jesus' suffering and death could be part of that plan. After the resurrection, he understood the meaning of the cross and lived out the Gospel boldly. If we—like Peter after the resurrection—can understand what it means to be saved by Jesus' death, we will have gone a long way in understanding the ways of God. We will also have a perspective from which to think about the death penalty today. It is not by taking life but by giving himself to and on behalf of sinners that Jesus is the Christ, our Messiah and Lord. When all seems lost, everything is gained. Lost in misery, we are given mercy. Despite our hatred, we receive love.

For Reflection and Discussion:

Watch the video clip of Vicki Schieber telling the story of the murder of her daughter Shannon. You can find it on the website of the Catholic Mobilizing Network (CMN). Go to the reading guide for this study: http://catholicsmobilizing.org/reading-guide/.

After listening to Vicki's story, think about the strange ways of God. Amid Vicki's suffering, she hears a call to serve. The call will help keep Shannon active for the good of the world. And this goodness has been a balm for Vicki.

God's Call of Love and Mercy

Consider God's word to Israel in the book of Isaiah: "For as the heavens are higher than the earth, / so are my ways higher than your ways, / my thoughts higher than your thoughts" (Isa 55:9). Chapter 55 of Isaiah is the end of a section (Isa 40–55) that proclaims God's mercy and redemption for his scattered people. God's mercy is awe-inspiring and mystifying. About fifty years earlier, Jerusalem was destroyed and the people exiled

to the great kingdom of Babylon. It seemed that the Jewish
people had lost everything: their land, the Jewish identity of
their descendants, and the very blessing of their Lord.[2] But at
the very time when they had been conquered by a foreign
empire, God called Israel to be a light to the nations. It was the
call given to Abraham, Moses, Joshua, and the kings of Israel
and Judah. Along with the land and a people, Abraham was
promised that "[a]ll the families of the earth will find blessing
in you" (Gen 12:3). When all seemed lost in Babylon, God's call
was renewed and intensified.

An essential part of God's grace is a call to us to be a light to
others. The self-giving grace of God is that we are grafted into
God's good work. We can see this pattern in the Old Testament
as well as the New. It is a pattern of salvation as vocation. It is
a call to live God's way of mercy and justice and to be a light to
the nations. This pattern is evident in the book of Isaiah, when
the prophet announces the return of the people from exile in
Babylon. "The LORD calls you back, / like a wife forsaken and
grieved in spirit . . . All your children shall be taught by the
LORD . . . In justice shall you be established" (Isa 54:6, 13, 14).
Notice that the return from exile means the renewal of the exiles
as God's covenant people: "Let the wicked forsake their way
. . . Let them turn to the LORD to find mercy . . . For my thoughts
are not your thoughts, / nor are your ways my ways" (Isa 55:7-8).
Finally, return of the Jews to Jerusalem is also a commission to
be the site for the gathering of all the peoples of the world. "The
foreigner joined to the LORD should not say, / 'The LORD will
surely exclude me from his people' . . . Them I will bring to my
holy mountain . . . For my house shall be called / a house of
prayer for all peoples" (Isa 56:3, 7).

This last line about the temple as "a house of prayer" is quoted
by Jesus when he enters the temple and denounces its use as
"a den of thieves" (Matt 21:13). A den of thieves is a place to
hide and conspire against others. A house of prayer is the opposite. It is a place of God's hospitality and grace. Because Jesus
is the Messiah, he enters the temple—the center of Israel's faith—

and he calls the people of God to its vocation. He calls them to be a light to the nations. Jesus turns over the tables of the money changers, but the issue is not just commerce in the temple. The issue is that the money changing is a sign of the boundary that has been set up between the temple and the world. Changing money in the temple is analogous to changing currency at the airport when coming home from a foreign country. Unclean coins of the world have to be changed to coins acceptable in the temple. The "den of thieves" is an allusion to Jeremiah 7:11 where Jeremiah denounces a belief that the temple is a bulwark against the world. In their den, thieves hide out and conspire against others. In cleansing the temple, Jesus claims authority over the temple and calls us to our mission to gather the nations, even our enemies.

Cleansing of the Temple

When Jesus cleanses the temple, his disciples' thoughts are drawn immediately to Psalm 69:10: "Zeal for your house will consume me" (John 2:17).

Pope Benedict XVI reflects on this passage in volume 2 of his *Jesus of Nazareth* (San Francisco: Ignatius Press, 2011).

Benedict compares Christ's zeal to his rejection of zealotry and insurrection against Rome. This rejection is implied in his accusation that the temple had become a "den of robbers."

Benedict explains, "The 'zeal' that would serve God through violence he transformed into the zeal of the Cross . . . the zeal of self-giving love. This zeal must become the Christian's goal" (22–23).

Jesus' cleansing of the temple is one trigger, among others, of the events that lead to the cross. Jesus' rejection in the temple (Matt 21:23-27), ironically, is also a renewal of the temple's purpose and of God's call in gathering the people of God. The temple had become a defense against a hostile world, and Jesus was announcing that it should be a gift to the world. Likewise, the cross was supposed to display Roman dominance—of the world's hostility to a Jewish Messiah—and God makes it a sign of his infinite mercy.

Jesus' death and resurrection are our salvation. As noted above, it is not the resurrection, but Jesus' death that is most confusing. The resurrection is certainly astounding and un-expected, but it confirms Jesus as Christ and Lord. The redeemer, however, is not supposed to be executed by the Romans. He is supposed to defeat the Roman oppressors and establish the kingdom of God. So, it is with cruel irony that Pontius Pilate, the Roman governor, executes Jesus under the title "the King of the Jews" (John 19:19-22). Pilate does not miss the opportunity to show his power. He uses the execution of one man to display the power of Rome over all Jews. The religious leaders want Jesus to be executed as a blasphemer, a messianic pretender, and a rebellious brigand. But Pilate crucifies him as Israel's forthright king. If a king represents a nation, Pilate uses Jesus' crucifixion to display Rome's domination of the Jews. But Pilate's cruel irony becomes, as we know, a joyous irony. The kingdom is established through God's self-giving suffering and death. God's ways are certainly not our ways.

Jesus' sacrifice is God's new covenant. The sin of Adam and Eve is that they do not trust God. They disobey. They want to be like gods, and to do so, they set themselves in competition with God. Again there is great irony. We, in our sin, set ourselves in competition with God, but God does not respond in kind. The original sin is that we try to grab for ourselves what God intends to share. We try to take for ourselves, but God continues to give. He gives himself to us for our redemption.

Our salvation comes as God responds to death with life. In Genesis 3, Adam and Eve believe the serpent when he tells them that God is withholding everything important from them. "God knows well that when you eat of it your eyes will be opened and you will be like gods" (Gen 3:5). The serpent makes it sound like God is against us, trying to keep us down. The opposite is revealed in Jesus' death. God is incarnate and with us in Jesus, and we set ourselves against him. We hope to kill God (although we do not see him as God). At the very moment when it seems that we strike out against God, God gives himself to us. At the moment when we have done all that we can to reject God, we find in the resurrection that nothing we can do can keep God from giving us new life in communion with him. In response to our violence and rejection, God gives mercy.

US Bishops' Statement on Capital Punishment

The United States Conference of Catholic Bishops holds that the call for abolition of the death penalty "sends a message that we can break the cycle of violence, that we need not take life for life."

It is "a manifestation of our belief in the unique worth and dignity of each person from the moment of conception, a creature made in the image and likeness of God."

It "is further testimony to our conviction . . . that God is indeed the Lord of life."

(www.usccb.org/issues-and-action/human-life-and-dignity/death
-penalty-capital-punishment/statement-on-capital-punishment.cfm)

For Reflection and Discussion:

Read Isaiah 54–56 and Jeremiah 7. Jesus quotes Isaiah 56:7 and Jeremiah 7:11 when he cleanses the temple. By reading the prophets Isaiah and Jeremiah, you will gain a sense of the power and profound meaning of Jesus' cleansing of the temple. Jesus' acts mean far more than a dislike for commercial enterprise in a worship place.

The temple has become a place of spiritual ownership and separation from the world. Like the people in biblical times, we often close ourselves up to protect ourselves against pain and persecution. But in the temple, Jesus calls us to hospitality for the world.

Reflect on our tendency to look to God as our defense. Reflect on ways that we can hear God's call to love and serve the world.

Capital Punishment

God's ways are not our ways. As we come to the conclusion of this chapter, please consider again the words of Pope Francis. He is quoted at length at the beginning of this chapter. The heart of his instruction to us is that salvation to new life is also our vocation. We are called to live what we have been given. Because God has first loved us, "we can move forward, boldly take the initiative, go out to others, seek those who have fallen away, stand at the crossroads and welcome the outcast." Because of God's infinite mercy, we can discover within ourselves "an endless desire to show mercy" (*Evangelii Gaudium* 24). New life in Christ means that we are gathered to be a light to the nations, to love as God loves, and to be just and merciful as God is just and merciful.

Prayer

"In the name of Jesus Christ crucified and risen, in the spirit of His messianic mission, enduring in the history of humanity, we raise our voices and pray that the Love which is in the Father may once again be revealed at this stage of history, and that, through the work of the Son and Holy Spirit, it may be shown to be present in our modern world and to be more powerful than evil: more powerful than sin and death" (John Paul II, *Dives in Misericordia* 15).

Given the call of the church to live out God's love, capital punishment is not a "side" issue. The church's stance against the death penalty comes from the heart of the gospel. In a statement issued in 1980, the United States Conference of Catholic Bishops observes "that abolition of the death penalty is most consonant with the example of Jesus, who both taught and practiced the forgiveness of injustice and who came 'to give his life as a ransom for many' " (Mark 10:45).[3] In effect, studying the church's stance against the death penalty is a way for us to understand our faith more deeply. Simply ignoring injustice is not the way. In God's love, justice and mercy meet. Therefore, the church's stance against the death penalty is a call for just punishment, but it is also a call for love and mercy. We are called to live the ways of God.

For Reflection and Discussion:

Read and discuss the 1980 statement by the United States Conference of Catholic Bishops (USCCB). It can be found at www .usccb.org/issues-and-action/human-life-and-dignity/death -penalty-capital-punishment/statement-on-capital-punishment .cfm. The statement is in five parts, with one section titled "Christian Values in the Abolition of Capital Punishment."

Key Points of Chapter 1

- For the followers of Jesus, his execution by the Romans seems to mean that he is not the Messiah. They scatter in fear and dismay.

- The crucifixion is the self-giving of God and consistent with who God is throughout Scripture. In explaining the loving mercy of God, the prophet Isaiah explains that God's ways are not our ways.

- In the face of violence and hatred, we often turn to vengeance and violent resistance.

- In contrast, Jesus Christ is God's loving response to human sin, opposition, and violence.

- The self-giving of God is the vocation of Israel and the church. The vocation is to be a light for the gathering of the peoples of the world.

- This call to be the gathering point is expressed in Jesus' cleansing of the temple in Jerusalem. The call is radical and part of the reason why Jesus is executed.

- Ironically, the cross, which is our attempt to reject God, becomes the medium for God's reconciliation for us and with us.

- Pope Francis notes that the call of the church is to live out this love and mercy that God gives to the world.

- The United States Conference of Catholic Bishops makes the connection between God's self-giving love in Jesus Christ and its stance against the death penalty.

2

Restorative Justice

When a conversation about capital punishment begins, it is inevitable that "an eye for an eye" will be discussed and defended. People know that the phrase is in the Bible. Usually, however, its place and purpose in Scripture is not known to those who use it to argue for the death penalty. The meaning of the phrase "an eye for an eye" seems obvious. It seems so obvious that its defenders do not make an effort to explain what it means. The phrase seems to mean that retribution is required to equal a crime: "a life for a life." In short, people commonly use "an eye for an eye" with the authority of Scripture, in order to defend retribution in kind. If I seriously injure or kill another, I must be seriously injured or killed. Given this common interpretation, it appears that retribution and vengeance are required by the Bible.

Consider a typical example. In recent years, executions by lethal injection have been botched, producing intense pain for the person being executed and a horrific experience for witnesses to the execution. State courts have been called to adjudicate legal challenges against lethal injection as cruel and unusual punishment.[1] In response to a botched execution in Ohio,[2] a reader of the Nashville daily the *Tennessean* writes,

13

> I say, why should we care? After all, I'm sure his victims suf-
> fered while he was killing them. The taking of life is wrong,
> no matter who does it. However, there is a biblical passage
> which reads "an eye for an eye," and I agree.[3]

The writer's use of the biblical "an eye for an eye" is typical. He proposes that the taking of life is wrong, but quickly he turns to the Bible to refute his own claim. In effect, he says that killing is wrong, however, the Bible says it is right. His use of "an eye for an eye" is typical in two ways. First, he cites the Bible as a higher authority while he takes the teaching out of the context of the Bible. Second, the biblical "an eye for an eye" is used to justify the suffering of a wrongdoer, here a murderer. The killer must not only be killed but also be killed in a way that produces suffering.

Restorative Justice

"Restorative justice focuses first on the victim and the community harmed by the crime . . . and insists that offenders
come to grips with the consequences of their actions. These
approaches are not 'soft on crime' because they specifically
call the offender to face victims and the communities. This
experience offers victims a much greater sense of peace and
accountability. Offenders who are willing to face the human
consequences of their actions are more ready to accept responsibility, make reparations, and rebuild their lives" (United States
Conference of Catholic Bishops, *Responsibility, Rehabilitation,
and Restoration*).

This chapter explains that this vengeful interpretation is incorrect. The biblical "an eye for an eye" does not command retribution in kind. In the context of biblical law, phrases like "an eye
for an eye, a tooth for a tooth" are meant to emphasize the grave
and terrible nature of maiming or killing another human being.
On this point, the writer of the editorial letter is correct. Taking
another person's life is wrong; maiming another is wrong. For

this reason, "an eye for an eye"—in the context of Old Testament law and the Jewish legal tradition—is used to emphasize the need for substantial and serious compensation to the victim. In the Old Testament, the death penalty is listed as punishment for certain crimes. For example, Leviticus 20:9 mandates: "Anyone who curses father or mother shall be put to death." Reading this passage should encourage us to pause to understand its aim and purpose. Obviously, something is intended other than its literal practice. On the whole, we will see that in the Old Testament killing a human being is so wrong that the biblical legal system sets up almost insurmountable roadblocks to carrying out a capital sentence. We will see that the Bible emphasizes restorative justice. It emphasizes the need to repair the harm done by sin. Restorative justice looks, first, to restore the victim, and it sees the restoration of the victim as the avenue for the true reformation of the offender.

Following God's Way of Restitution

God's saving work of reconciliation and the restoration of human life is the proper context for the injunction "an eye for an eye, a tooth for a tooth." This proper context was developed in chapter 1: the call to follow God's way is the proper framework for understanding the laws of the Old Testament—the laws of the Torah. (The Torah is the first five books of the Bible: Genesis, Exodus, Leviticus, Numbers, and Deuteronomy.[4]) The Torah is the law of life for the Jewish people. After God liberates the Hebrew people from slavery in Egypt (the exodus), the Lord gathers them at Mount Sinai. The Lord establishes a covenant with the people and, through the covenant, God calls Israel to be holy as God is holy, to be a kingdom of priests (Exod 19:6). For the Hebrew people, God's law reveals his justice and mercy. In this sense, the law is a gift. It is a gift that God calls Israel to live out God's justice and mercy for the world to see.

Within the context of God's law and Israel's vocation, we will consider specifically Exodus 21:22-24 and Leviticus 24:17-20. These passages are often used to justify vengeance and to promote

capital punishment. They are referred to as the "law of talion"—
lex talionis—or the law of retaliation. You might have learned
that this law of retaliation was used by the early Babylonians to
limit retaliation and to nip blood feuds in the bud.[5] In this case,
the meaning of the law of talion would be "take *only* an eye for
an eye." In ancient Babylonian law, this limit on vengeance
seems to be the purpose of "an eye for an eye, a life for a life."
The *lex talionis* is borrowed by the ancient Israelites, but in the
context of the Torah and God's covenant, the phrase takes on a
different meaning. Looking at the passages carefully, we will
find that they do not promote vengeance or retribution.

Rejection of Vengeance

"Particular commands like the one found in Genesis 9:6—'If
anyone sheds the blood of man, by man shall his blood be
shed'—have a poetic character that indicates an original purpose . . . removed from the sphere of literal legal applications.

The Jewish Scriptures and the teachings of Jesus Christ as a
whole esteem the protection of human life, the practice of mercy
and the rejection of vengeance" (Archbishop Wilton D. Gregory,
"The Church's Evolving View on the Death Penalty," *Origins*
38, no. 23 [November 2008]).

At first glance, you will wonder how the *lex talionis* passages
can be anything but a call for retribution. Consider the three
passages:

> When men have a fight and hurt a pregnant woman . . . [I]f
> injury ensues, you shall give life for life, eye for eye, tooth
> for tooth, hand for hand, foot for foot, burn for burn, wound
> for wound, stripe for stripe. (Exod 21:22-24)

> Whoever takes the life of any human being shall be put to
> death; whoever takes the life of an animal shall make restitu-
> tion of another animal, life for a life. (Lev 24:17-18)

Anyone who inflicts a permanent injury on his or her neighbor shall receive the same in return: fracture for fracture, eye for eye, tooth for tooth. (Lev 24:19-20)

Are these passages consistent with the restorative justice and mercy of God? Such a claim does not seem likely at this juncture. But consider that Jesus announces that he comes to fulfill the law (Matt 5:17). If Jesus fulfills rather than rejects the law, a proper understanding of the biblical "an eye for an eye" will be consistent with Jesus' own reaction when confronted with the death penalty. Jesus is asked to confirm a law that seems to require stoning of a woman caught in adultery (Deut 22:22). Instead, he tells the woman, "Go, [and] from now on do not sin any more" (John 8:11). In this event, Jesus is not rejecting the law but following it to the fullest extent. Likewise, the Old Testament passages that seem to require retribution do not. They are consistent with the vocation of Israel and the church to live in a new way of justice and mercy as they follow the ways of God.

God's call to us can be put in terms of a vocation of restorative justice—of a call to restore brokenness rather than to destroy the sinful person. This call is the heart of Jesus' words to the woman caught in adultery. The purpose of phrases like "life for a life, eye for an eye" is to point to the gravity of injuring or killing another person. The purpose is to require rigorous accountability and to reinforce the obligation of restitution to the victims and their families. In reference to Exodus 21:22-25, the notes of *The Catholic Study Bible* explain that "the law of talion is not held up as a general principle to be applied throughout the book of the covenant."[6] The application of it in Exodus 21:22-25 is to require "rigorous accountability aimed to prevent injury to a woman about to give birth." The same rigorous accountability includes a call to restore those victimized by the crime.

In short, restoration is the goal. The notes in *The Catholic Study Bible* in reference to Leviticus 24:19-20 parallel the explanations given for Exodus 21:22-25. They explain that the so-called law of talion can be understood "to mean that monetary compensation equal to the injury is to be paid."[7] In other words, the phrase "eye for an eye" is not to be taken literally as retaliation. Similar figurative language is used in Matthew 5:29. "If your right eye causes you to sin, tear it out and throw it away." The meaning of this phrase is not literal. According to *The Catholic Study Bible*, it means that "no sacrifice is too great to avoid total destruction."[8] Likewise, in terms of personal injury or death, "an eye for an eye" means that no recompense—no sacrifice of restitution on the part of the offender—is too great. Compensation must be given, but the offender is called also to seek forgiveness and atone for the wrongs done. "A life for a life" indicates that someone who kills another must give all of his or her life over to the restitution of the victims.

For Reflection and Discussion:

In 1973, Marietta Jaeger-Lane was on a camping trip with her family when her seven-year-old daughter, Susie, was kidnapped, assaulted, and murdered. None of the details of the abduction were known until a year later when Marietta played the key role in identifying and arresting the killer. Since then and after years of struggle and pain, she has been an activist on the campaign to abolish the death penalty.

View a video clip of Marietta telling her story. It can be found on the CMN website at http://catholicsmobilizing.org/reading -guide/. In the clip, Marietta engages in debate about the Bible.

Reflect on the reasons given for each point of view—Marietta's view that her stance is based in her faith, and her opponents' view that their opinions are based on the Bible.

"A Life for a Life" in Context

How can this be? How can a biblical teaching ("life for life") that seems to so obviously require retaliation actually be about restitution? Richard Buck, in *Where Justice and Mercy Meet*, explains the passages from a Jewish perspective. The first point to make is that a long history of Jewish interpretation recognizes the implausibility of literal retribution. Two thousand years ago, a preeminent rabbi asked, "What happens to a blind person who injures another person's eyes?"[9] Consider this line of thought. If a man who is fighting injures a bystander and causes a miscarriage, will the man have to wait till his own wife is pregnant to cause her to miscarry? What if the man is not married? On this point, Exodus 21:22 offers the answer, which is "the guilty one shall be fined as much as the woman's husband demands of him." This call for compensation parallels the meaning of "an eye for an eye" (which follows in vv. 23-24). The phrase has a particular meaning within the biblical legal system, which emphasizes restitution.

Richard Buck shows that the biblical use of "an eye for an eye" emphasizes the seriousness of compensation. In the Torah, "an eye for an eye" is applied to personal injury, while a straightforward call for compensation is applied to the loss of property (e.g., a cow for a cow):

> By using the language "an eye for an eye" the Hebrew Scriptures mean to make clear that injuring another person's body is a much more serious crime than damaging another person's property. . . . Without the severe "an eye for an eye," the severity of the harm and the need for compassion for the victim is lost. Imagine how the Scriptures might be read if they stated explicitly that one who injures another's body must make financial restitution. . . . We might wonder why the restitution required for the more serious offense of personal injury is no greater than that required for property damage.[10]

In effect, the law of talion, when set within the Torah, does not require literal retribution, but uses severe language to emphasize the seriousness of the crime, to necessitate rigorous accountability, and to impose the obligation of restitution in the strongest possible terms.

Because taking another person's life is such a grave matter, Torah law imposes the death penalty for killing another person, but—also because taking another life is so grave—it imposes considerable barriers to actually carrying out capital punishment. According to Richard,

> First, the Hebrew Scriptures do require that the death penalty be imposed for certain crimes. Second, the prerequisites that must be met before the death penalty is imposed are so difficult to meet that it was nearly impossible for any offender to be executed. This second point is consistent with the first.[11]

The two points are consistent because killing a person is always awful. Look back at the inconsistency of the writer of the editorial letter, cited at the beginning of this chapter. He writes, "The taking of life is wrong, no matter who does it. However, there is a biblical passage which reads 'an eye for an eye,' and I agree." In effect, he says, "it is wrong, but it is right." He contradicts himself. In contrast, the biblical approach is much more consistent: it imposes the death penalty because murder is so grave, but also puts in place almost insurmountable barriers to its implementation, also because killing is so grave.

Innocence and the Death Penalty

Between 1973 and 2013, 143 people have been freed from death row because of their innocence. They have been acquitted; charges related to the crime have been dismissed by the prosecution, or they have been granted a complete pardon based on evidence of innocence.

From 1973 to 1999, there was an average of 3.03 exonerations per year. From 2000 to 2013, there was an average of 4.29 exonerations per year.

The average time in prison for the false conviction is 10.6 years.

(Death Penalty Information Center, www.deathpenaltyinfo.org /innocence-and-death-penalty)

These barriers—the prerequisites for actual death sentence—pertain to the quantity and quality of witnesses, burdens of justice placed upon the witnesses, very high standards of proof, and requirements that a potential offender is due advanced warning. Some hold that these requirements for the use of the death penalty are, in practice, impossible to meet. In any case, Richard Buck emphasizes that there is clear disapproval in the tradition for actually carrying out the death penalty. He cites the Mishnah (the "oral law"): "Rabbi Tarfon and Rabbi Akiva say: Had we been on the Sanhedrin [at the time when they still performed executions] no person would ever have been executed."[12] For this reason, many raise the question whether or not the death penalty as it is prescribed in the Bible can make any sense apart from the entirety of the Torah and the practices of a Sanhedrin (a Jewish court). An application of the Hebrew Bible as a recommendation for capital punishment in the United States today is not only misleading but also irresponsible.[13]

For Reflection and Discussion:

The barriers to the use of the death penalty, in Jewish law, have a foundation in principles of faith as well as in practice.

We have seen that, as a matter of faith in the Lord of life, our biblical faith puts up barriers to our taking of life. This point will be covered in chapter 3, which will discuss Jesus' response to the proposed stoning of the woman caught in adultery (John 8:2-11). Jesus, in his subtle words and actions, reminds the crowd gathered for the stoning of the requirement of the law.

In practical terms, many people hold that there should be no recourse to the death penalty if even one innocent person might be executed. One such person is Sam Millsap. As a district attorney in Austin, Texas (first elected in 1982), Sam successfully convicted several murderers and secured the sentence of death by lethal injection. After discovering that a few of those executed were innocent, Sam started to oppose the death penalty (www .texasafterviolence.org/sam-millsap.aspx).

Consider Sam's view by listening to his story. A video clip can be found at http://catholicsmobilizing.org/reading-guide/.

Restorative Justice

If you were to talk to most people about "an eye for an eye," they would ask, How can it be? How can a biblical teaching that requires the death penalty ("a life for a life") turn out to be virtually impossible to impose in practice? How can you manage to find restitution and mercy in the "eye for an eye" of the Bible? These questions are made clear in the video clip about Marietta Jaeger-Lane, which was suggested at the end of the first section of this chapter. Some people are appalled by her arguments against the death penalty. Her own daughter was murdered, but she is accused of "distorting Scripture" and putting a "liberal spin" on it. But Marietta knows intuitively what we have learned in this chapter: If taking a life is an incredibly grave matter, then taking a life as punishment is equally grave. The meaning of "an eye for an eye" is shaped within Israel's covenant and call. The redemption of Israel—God's way of restoration and mercy—is also Israel's vocation to follow in God's way and to be a light to the nations. We are called to live out the justice and the mercy of God. In this context, "an eye for an eye" does not encourage revenge, but directs us to the restoration of the victim.

Salvation is a vocation to live in God's way and to practice God's restorative justice. When the Hebrew people are enslaved in Egypt, Pharaoh is like a god. He rules over all aspects of life including questions of life and death. Through his contest with the God of Israel—through the plagues and flight of the Hebrews through the Red Sea—the pharaoh is defeated. He does not even rule his own heart (Exod 9:12). But the surprising, gracious, and awe-inspiring fact about the God of Israel is not only that he is more powerful than Pharaoh but also that he does not rule like a pharaoh. God invites the people into covenant, an unconditional covenant to which he binds himself for the good of the people and all of creation. He invites the people to bind themselves to each other through the law given at Mount Sinai: God's law and God's way.

The covenant and its way of life (its law) mean that Israel will never need a pharaoh. God—whose ways are not pharaoh's way or the ways of the nations—is their king. If you read the books of Samuel, Kings, and Chronicles, you will see that the downfall of Israel and its kings is based on this point. The monarchs sin when they act like pharaohs, and the people falter when they disregard God as their true king. The people of the covenant are called to be set apart, to be a light to the nations, "a kingdom of priests, a holy nation" (Exod 19:6). Within this context, the death penalty is required in the Torah and, because of the Torah, it is virtually impossible to put into practice. It is required because God is the giver of life; no pharaoh can claim God's prerogative. It is virtually impossible to perform for precisely the same reason. God's ways are not pharaoh's ways. God is the giver of life. Pharaoh takes and destroys; God restores us to life.

A Prayer for Mercy

"Let us accept the grace of Christ's Resurrection! Let us be renewed by God's mercy, let us be loved by Jesus, let us enable the power of his love to transform our lives too; and let us become agents of this mercy, channels through which God can water the earth, protect all creation and make justice and peace flourish.

"And so we ask the risen Jesus, who turns death into life, to change hatred into love, vengeance into forgiveness, war into peace" (Pope Francis, *Urbi et Orbi* Message, Easter 2013).

For Reflection and Discussion:

Read Exodus 21:12-37. Notice the frequent interchange between three kinds of punishments: (1) compensation to the injured party, (2) the death sentence, and (3) phrases like "eye for eye." The use of these kinds of punishments does not always seem consistent. For example, killing a slave might not require punishment at all (v. 21), but cursing one's parents merits death (v. 17). Causing a miscarriage requires compensation, but if the woman is also burned in the accident, then "burn for burn" is required.

Read the passage again and consider the forms of punishment, not as literal acts, but as pointers to the gravity of the crime and the importance of redress. Does the passage seem more consistent and reasonable?

Key Points of Chapter 2

- "An eye for an eye," the so-called law of talion, is not understood within the Hebrew Scriptures as requiring retribution. In context, it points to the severity of personal injury and the serious need for restitution of the victim.

- The Mosaic law requires the death penalty for some crimes, especially taking of life. But, for the same reason, the law makes the practical application of the death penalty extremely difficult. Legal provisions about the testimony of witnesses and the burden of proof makes actually meting out a penalty of death virtually impossible.

- The Jewish legal tradition is against the death penalty in attitude and practice.

- Many Jewish scholars question whether the Jewish law on the death penalty can have any application in a secular court system.

- The emphasis on restoration (rather than retribution) fits with Israel's covenant with God and call to be a light to the nations. Restoration is a fundamental theme of Scripture.

- In Matthew 5:17, Jesus states that he comes to fulfill the law. In this sense, Jesus makes God's restoration of human life a reality, and he calls us to follow him, to live out his way of reconciliation.

3

Responding to Evil with Good

Jesus instructs his disciples and followers to forgo vengeance and retaliation. At the beginning of the Gospel of Matthew (chaps. 5–7), Jesus teaches from a mountainside. In the Sermon on the Mount, he calls us to be merciful and righteous, to be peacemakers, to be instruments of God's reconciliation and hospitality to the world. Jesus proclaims,

> You have heard that it was said, "An eye for an eye and a tooth for a tooth." But I say to you, offer no resistance to one who is evil. When someone strikes you on (your) right cheek, turn the other one to him as well. (Matt 5:38-39)

Likewise, Jesus exhorts his disciples to love their enemies. "[L]ove your enemies, and pray for those who persecute you" (Matt 5:44). Jesus is the incarnation of God. For this reason, Jesus not only teaches but also embodies his teachings throughout his life and especially in his death.

Consider that Jesus does not resist when he is arrested in the Garden of Gethsemane. When temple guards and chief priests arrive, one of the disciples, Peter (according to John 18:10), strikes a servant of the high priest and cuts off his ear. Jesus immediately heals the servant (Luke 22:51). The scene is remarkable; Jesus' actions are astounding. At the moment when he is suffering injustice, at the moment when he is betrayed and falsely arrested—betrayed by a kiss (Luke 22:48) and arrested under the cover of night (Luke 22:53)—at that moment, Jesus heals a member of the arresting delegation. Jesus answers darkness with light.

Realistically, it is hard to imagine any of us doing the same, especially if we were faced with a false arrest. Obviously, you and I are not likely to heal—by a simple touch—a member of the arresting force. But beyond the miraculous, there is more about Jesus' loving response that seems very hard, perhaps impossible to achieve. In our lives, returning evil with good does not seem to achieve anything good. We just suffer the injury and injustice. Jesus refuses to retaliate against those who arrest, accuse, convict, and cry out for his crucifixion. But his refusal accomplishes our salvation. His way of nonretaliation puts into place God's loving answer to our rejection of God (which is the root of our sin). Jesus' way of peace accomplishes something good.

Radical Forgiveness

Antoinette Bosco's son and daughter-in-law were murdered in 1993. In her book *Radical Forgiveness* (Maryknoll, NY: Orbis, 2009), she reflects upon the terrible experience:

"If Jesus gave us no explanation for why evil continues to have power, he did give us a blueprint for dealing with it. 'Overcome evil with good' . . . is, I believe, the only way to flourish in a world where evil, from the beginning, has taken up residence. I know from experience that Jesus' approach, which puts good into practice, is better than getting lost in a web of 'gaping holes.' "

Is such a way possible for us? And if it is, what does nonretaliation mean for our response to those who commit murder? Do we let the offender go free? These questions about nonretaliation form the topic of this chapter. When faced with murder, we seem to have two contrasting options: either justice or mercy. Either we call for justice, which, for many of us, includes a call for the death penalty; or we call for mercy, which seems to mean clemency or exoneration. Mercy seems to mean that we "forgive and forget" and do not face up to the evil at all. We will consider a third option. We will consider the possibility of following Jesus' teachings of nonretaliation—about really responding with good—as a means of confronting evil and calling a stop to it. At the end, this chapter will make a connection between Jesus' Sermon on the Mount and imposing, upon a convicted murderer, a severe prison sentence—for the murderer's own good, in hope that the person will turn his or her life around.

The Fullness of the Law

When trying to understand the Sermon on the Mount and its difficult teachings, we should avoid letting ourselves or an offender off the hook too easily. There are several ways to let ourselves off the hook. For example, when we read Matthew 5:39, "offer no resistance to one who is evil," we might be tempted to narrow its application. Perhaps the teaching is only meant for priests and religious sisters and brothers, nuns and monks. They, for example, are exempt from fighting in war and from other uses of force. Or we might take another approach: perhaps the call for nonresistance does not apply for today, but to the kingdom of God that has yet to come. "Certainly," we might say, "Jesus' instructions are not about practical matters of living in the real world." We might conclude that the merciful and the peacemakers (Matt 5:5, 9) are irrelevant in the real world, but they will receive a reward in heaven. These are ways of letting *ourselves* off the hook. But we might also be too easy on those who persecute, oppress, or kill others. We might hold that the

Sermon on the Mount applies to our lives completely and, there-fore, "offer no resistance to one who is evil" means that there is no punishment for criminal offenders.

This part of the book makes the case for nonretaliation as a different kind of option. The first step in understanding Jesus' call for nonretaliation is to understand the proper meaning of "an eye for an eye." We discovered, in chapter 2, that phrases like "a tooth for a tooth" and "a life for a life" are often used in the Old Testament to establish the magnitude of both culpability and responsibility. If one were to maim or kill another, one's guilt is serious and one's burden of compensation for victims and their families is unimaginably great. If I were to kill your cow, then I ought to give you another cow. If my irresponsibility were to cripple you, I ought to compensate you "a leg for a leg." You might respond, "You will never be able to compensate me for the loss of my lost leg. And your leg is going to do me no good." And that's the point. The burden on me is almost too great to imagine.

In contrast, the popular (but not biblical) interpretation of the *lex talionis* ("an eye for an eye") emphasizes retribution in kind. But people who hold this view seldom think it through. The popular view holds that if the victim suffers, the offender must suffer the same. But quickly, this view starts to unravel. Suppose I lost a leg in an accident caused by a drunk driver. Can I expect the courts to rule that the offender's leg is to be amputated? And if the leg is amputated, what am I supposed to do with it? Usually—hopefully—the courts require some kind of jail time for the offender, in hope that the person will realize the severity of the crime and begin to live a new way. Required drug and alcohol counseling and a rehabilitation program would be ap-propriate as well. Also, I would expect appropriate monetary compensation, not only for hospital bills but also for lost income and suffering. This is the biblical view of "a leg for a leg." It emphasizes the severity of the crime and the offender's mo-mentous responsibility for the restoration of the victims and their families.

In chapter 2, we also considered the barriers in the Jewish legal system to actually using capital punishment. These "barriers"—such as requirements and responsibilities of witnesses—are not meant to benefit criminals but to promote justice and righteousness. As a comparison, consider that people today often complain that death row inmates are allowed too many appeals. When people complain they say silly things like, "get rid of all the appeals because murderers don't deserve it." But even if they don't, we do. We deserve to have a legal process that is just and is set up to root out its own injustice. Think in these terms when you consider the Sermon on the Mount—Jesus' call to love our enemies and to return evil with good. We are called to live with justice, and the injustice of another does not give us permission to disregard who we are called to be.

Consider the account, in John 8:2-11, of the woman caught in adultery. When you read the passage, you will notice that the woman has not been tried or sentenced in the Jewish court. The Sanhedrin, the Jewish court, would be responsible for hearing the case of the woman caught in adultery. You may recall that it hears the case against Jesus at the end of the gospels. For the woman caught in adultery, there is not even a veneer of an official gathering. Rather than a court case, the scene has a tone of vigilante justice. A crowd gathers around Jesus in "the temple area" (John 8:2). Some scribes and the Pharisees bring a woman before Jesus so that he will be her judge. Their tactics have a cynical undertone. Scribes and Pharisees want Jesus to judge the woman's case in terms of Torah law, but they are really looking to judge him. Will he reject the law for the sake of mercy? Will he reject mercy for the sake of the law? His opponents have him in a situation where any answer he gives will be wrong in some way.

Jesus, as usual, gives an interesting and unexpected response. He refers to the righteousness of the law. He refers implicitly to the traditions of Jewish legal practice in terms of the righteousness that Torah law requires. Jesus shows mercy, not by backing away from the law, but by applying the righteousness of the law to accusers, witnesses, and offender. The scribes and Pharisees claim that the laws of Moses require that the woman be stoned. But Jesus turns their attention first not to her but to her accusers and their witnesses. The witnesses, by law, are required to cast the first stones (John 8:7; Deut 17:7[1]). This requirement brings to mind the importance of the commandment against bearing false witness (Exod 20:16).

In the Jewish tradition, the commandment against false witness points to a whole host of requirements and responsibilities set upon witnesses. Consider Exodus 23:1: "Do not join your hand with the wicked to be a witness supporting violence."[2] The command is parallel to Jesus' words to those who gather to stone the woman: "Let the one among you who is without sin be the first to throw a stone at her" (John 8:7). Here, "without sin" can be taken to mean something like, "Who has not been corrupted by this very gathering to stone this woman?" The woman's accusers take a narrow slice of the law, proof-texting the portion pertaining only to her. But Jesus reminds them of the law's full requirements—pertaining to the whole of Torah and the righteousness of the people as a whole. He gives them time to think by drawing in the sand. They get the point and silently slip away. After they disperse, Jesus now turns the righteousness of the law to the woman: "Go, [and] from now on do not sin any more" (John 8:11).

John Paul II on Punishment

"Public authority must redress the violation of personal and social rights by imposing on the offender an adequate punishment for the crime, as a condition for the offender to regain the exercise of his or her freedom. In this way authority also fulfils the purpose of defending public order and ensuring people's safety, while at the same time offering the offender an incentive and help to change his or her behavior and be rehabilitated" (*Evangelium Vitae* 56).

In sum, mercy fulfills justice. (1) The fact that "an eye for an eye" is about not primarily retribution but compensation does not mean that it is "easy." For a person who kills another, the *lex talionis*—"an eye for an eye" as retribution—means death. But the mercy of requiring compensation (rather than death) does not mean that the offender gets off easy. The offender must live to restore what cannot be restored. The burden is great. The person will never be able to do enough. But it is a burden that opens the possibility for acting meaningfully and deeply for another. (2) In Jesus' encounter with the woman caught in adultery, we see a seamless call for righteousness. The fact that the biblical legal system makes the death penalty almost impossible to be put to practice does not mean that it disregards justice. On the contrary, its call for righteousness applies to all and the whole people of God. One person's terrible act of killing another does not give us permission to do evil to the killer.

These two points offer insight into Jesus' Sermon on the Mount (Matt 5–7). As he begins the lengthy set of instructions, Jesus announces that he has "come not to abolish but to fulfill [the law]" (Matt 5:17). In this regard, his teachings against retaliation and retribution are fully consistent with the Hebrew Scriptures. The purpose of law is for the people to live together, under God, in peace and justice and to be "the salt of the earth" (Matt 5:13).

For Reflection and Discussion:

The teachings of the church hold that punishment should be medicinal and "contribute to the correction of the guilty party" (*Catechism of the Catholic Church* 2266). But often, we say that we want to see murderers suffer immeasurably. We do not think through the implications of what we say. Consider the view and experiences of Anthony Graves.

Anthony was falsely convicted of murder in 1994 and sentenced to death by lethal injection. He spent eighteen years in prison, sixteen of those in solitary confinement, twelve on death row. His conviction was overturned in 2006, but he waited retrial in solitary confinement for four more years. Finally, in 2010, his case was dismissed because, according to the district attorney, "He's an innocent man. . . . There is nothing that connects Anthony Graves to this crime."[3]

In June 2012, Anthony testified before the US Senate Judiciary Hearing on solitary confinement. You will find a clip of his testimony on the CMN website at http://catholicsmobilizing.org /reading-guide/.

View the video and reflect on Anthony's description of life in solitary confinement. His testimony is passionate and troubling. Please thoughtfully consider Anthony's final statement that "solitary confinement dehumanizes us all."

Turn the Other Cheek

Jesus' teachings against retaliation and violence and for the love of enemies make clear that the death penalty has no purpose in our call, as Christians, to follow in the ways of God. The point becomes even clearer if we consider Jesus' arrest, trial, and crucifixion. Deuteronomy 19:19 seems to put the right of retaliation in the hands of Jesus. "[Y]ou shall do to the false witness just as that false witness planned to do to the other." It seems that Jesus would have the right of retaliation. Instead, he says on the cross, "Father, forgive them, they know not what they do" (Luke 23:34). Jesus accepts his death and its injustice, and he does not wish death on those who are responsible.

While Jesus calls for love of enemies and nonretaliation, it is not always obvious what these teachings imply. Do we ignore injustice? Do we accept the wrongdoing of our enemies? To approach an answer, we should begin with this basic point: If Jesus fulfills the law, he completes its call for justice as well as for mercy and reconciliation. Therefore, the answer to the question Do we ignore injustice? will have to be no. We ought not to ignore wrongdoing, certainly not horrific crimes. However, we usually think of "turn the other cheek" as the invitation to be passive—to bear injustice silently, without notice or complaint. Reading the Sermon on the Mount, it is hard to think otherwise. Consider the passage once again:

> But I say to you, offer no resistance to one who is evil. When someone strikes you on (your) right cheek, turn the other one to him as well. If anyone wants to go to law with you over your tunic, hand him your cloak as well. Should anyone press you into service for one mile, go with him for two miles. (Matt 5:39-41)

Although it might seem unlikely, this passage offers a way to deal directly and constructively with evil, especially for those who experience helplessness—the helplessness that often comes from suffering terrible injustices.

In the teachings of Jesus, nonretaliation is a way to avoid passivity, to take action by doing what is good, and to call the offender to account by highlighting his or her injustice. Consider that Matthew 5:39-41, cited above, is preceded by, "You have heard that it was said, 'An eye for an eye and a tooth for a tooth'" (5:38). The phrasing, "You have heard it said . . . But I say to you," means not that Jesus is overturning the laws of Moses, but that he is calling his disciples "to follow the logical trajectory of a commandment's purpose and to act on it."[4] In other words, Jesus' follow up, "But I say to you," means not that Jesus is going to say the opposite, but that he is going to say something further.

With his "But I say," Jesus is going to take us a step further toward the fulfillment of the law. "But I say to you, offer no resistance to one who is evil" takes the original teaching further. If "an eye for an eye" has the purpose of addressing wrongs primarily through compensation and restoration, its fulfillment depends upon the compliance of the offender. In effect, the law—rightfully—is concerned with what the offender, the criminal must do. With his teaching, "offer no resistance to one who is evil," Jesus completes this law of restoration by recommending action for the ones who are wronged, regardless of their power to change the offender.

Regardless of the acts of the offender, we can take action. A violent offender may be unrepentant, but the victim—as hard as it is—can still act righteously. This just response is implied in the phrase "turn the other cheek." A slap on the right cheek was an insult in the ancient world—an act to demean and to establish the inferiority of the one who is slapped. Such a slap sends a message. People with social status will often justify hitting inferiors because they are inferior, blaming them for the violence that they suffer. Members of the dominant class believe that their power gives them the right. Consider the history of racism in the United States or the reasons given, in a chauvinist atmosphere, when men strike out against women. In this context, men will say, "She should not have made me so mad" or "She deserved it." Usually, in such a situation, hitting back is not an option. Hitting back is exactly the kind of response that the abuser understands and knows that he can win.

"Should anyone press you into service for one mile, go with him for two miles" (Matt 5:41). In Jesus' time, this "anyone" would be a Roman soldier. The imperial soldier could require, by law and by force, a Jew in conquered Palestine to do his bidding. Here, striking back at the soldier would not be an option. Jesus recommends, instead, that the person impressed into service is able to make a decision of his or her own. He or she can do more than the soldier requires. He can change the oppression into willing service. You might ask, "What difference does this contrast make—between oppression and willing service? Either way, the Jew has to carry the soldier's burden." In terms of the call of the gospel, there is a world of difference. On the one hand, oppression is suffering an evil. On the other hand, responding by going over what is required puts the oppressed in charge. He or she gives the oppressor a gift. A person's good actions, rather than the oppressor's evil, has the last word.

Likewise, turning the cheek is a way to respond with good. It is not cowering and hiding. It is not backing down. It is an action. It is different than the two typical responses: either running away or striking back. As a third option, turning the other cheek is standing up straight so that the injustice can be seen plainly. It gives us a way to stand face-to-face and toe-to-toe with someone who has wronged us. According to New Testament scholar N. T. Wright, "Hitting back only keeps the evil in circulation. Offering the other cheek implies: hit me again if you like, but now as an equal, not an inferior."[5] Hit me again, but I will not allow you to think that the action is something that I accept. Your act is unjust. Turning the other cheek is a way to refuse to allow the offender to shape the world and how we will act in it. It is responding to evil with good.

"I have concluded that forgiveness is a paradox: we cannot heal ourselves if we do not forgive others, but if we do forgive, it is we ourselves who benefit the most. If we let feelings of hatred and revenge consume us when we are devastatingly hurt, we cease to be the human beings we were created to be. We condemn ourselves to live in anguish.

"I think that's what Jesus meant when he told us we must overcome evil with good" (Antoinette Bosco, *Choosing Mercy: A Mother of Murder Victims Pleads to End the Death Penalty* [Maryknoll, NY: Orbis, 2001], 56).

What good is that? you might ask. What good is it to take more abuse? Certainly, Jesus is not recommending that we take more abuse. Turning the other cheek is a means of action in a terrible situation over which the victim has no control. It might not make sense at first. And I admit that it does not entirely make sense to me now; I have not experienced the evil of having a loved one murdered. But I do know that people have experienced the wonder of turning the other cheek at horrific times in their lives. A moving example is provided by Antoinette Bosco,[6] who had to reckon with the brutal murder of her son and daughter-in-law. She tells the story of her hatred, pain, and confusion in the months following the murders. After much struggle, she realized that her inability to forgive bound her to the killer in a ruinous way. Forgiveness allowed her to face the evil straight on and to take control of her own life—no longer controlled by the evil acts of the murderer.[7] For Antoinette, forgiveness was a way to "turn the other cheek," to stand up for herself, to take control of a situation that was controlled by the killer. It was a way to restore goodness to her life.

For Reflection and Discussion:

Consider the stories of Theresa Hoffman and Vicki Cox, who have family members who were murdered. Through their experiences they found healing in forgiveness and in focusing on love for their loved ones rather than hate for the killer. You will find video clips of Theresa and Vicki telling their stories on the CMN website at http://catholicsmobilizing.org/reading -guide/.

Loving Our Enemies

Like "turning the other cheek," loving our enemies and those who persecute us is not passive. It is taking action for the good (Matt 5:43-48). Love is not necessarily liking a person, and it is certainly not accepting another person's sinful actions. Love is wanting and working for another person's good. It is seeing the goodness of others (even when they might not see it themselves!). Sometimes we have to look beyond the surface of corruption and evil. Sometimes we see only malice and hatred from others, and we have to trust in their goodness as an image of God. In trusting God's goodness, we are called to work for the good of our enemies and those who have hurt us. We do not have to like them. We do not have to accept what they do or have done. Like "turning the other cheek," love is assertive and does not ignore the wrongs done. Mercy does not contradict justice. Mercy means wanting another person to be free of his or her own injustice. And to be free of it, the injustice cannot be overlooked. It has to be faced straight on.

For this reason, activists against the death penalty—including families of murder victims and often the families of murderers—want grave prison sentences for convicted killers. In line with Jesus' teachings on nonretaliation, calling for a weighty and momentous prison sentence is a way to avoid passivity, to take action by doing what is good, and to call the offender to account by standing against his or her injustice. Serious and substantial prison time is required to match the gravity of the crime. These family members of murder victims hope that conditions of imprisonment will be humane. They hope that through incarceration some goodness will grow within the offenders, some desire for the restoration of the victims' families, some sense that what they have done can never be made right. But these hopes are out of the control of victims' families and society as a whole. As Antoinette Bosco has realized, we do have control over the goodness that comes from us. We can restore and sustain goodness in our lives.

Resistance to Evil

The perspective of the Murder Victims' Families for Reconciliation (MVFR) parallels the gospel-basis of the civil rights movement.

Consider the description offered by Martin Luther King Jr. in his *Stride Toward Freedom* (Boston: Beacon Press, 2010):

"Nonviolent resistance is not a method for cowards; it does resist . . .

[It] is directed against forces of evil rather than against persons who happen to be doing the evil . . .

[It] avoids not only external physical violence but also internal violence of spirit . . .

It is based on the conviction that the universe is on the side of justice" (90–92).

Consider the statements made by Murder Victims' Families for Reconciliation (MVFR). The members define reconciliation as "accepting that you cannot undo the murder but you can decide how you want to live afterwards."[8] The organization is against the death penalty for the following reasons:[9]

- "The death penalty distracts the public and the judicial system from the more important issues of what victims' families and their communities need to heal and become safer."

- "The death penalty diverts resources, 100's of millions of dollars, into the capital system—resources that could be spent to help families with expenses such as funeral costs, daily needs while grieving, resources to aid with healing, sending children of murder victims to college, and providing communities with resources to prevent violent crimes before they happen."

- "The death penalty often causes huge divisions within communities, within victims' groups, and even within victims' families at a time when families and communities need to support each other the most."

- "The death penalty delays justice and it delays the healing process. Capital cases often take 25 years or more to reach completion, all the while keeping victims' families stuck in the system much longer than is the case with noncapital trials."

- "The death penalty causes damage to the families of the persons executed. Many of our members feel strongly about not causing further damage, pain, and suffering to these families and their communities."

This perspective of murder victims' families accord with teachings of Jesus, as they are remembered by St. Paul when he instructs the church in Rome: "Do not repay anyone evil for evil. . . . Do not be conquered by evil but conquer evil with good" (Rom 12:17, 21).

The Peace Prayer of St. Francis

O Divine Master,
Grant that I may not so much seek
To be consoled, as to console;
To be understood, as to understand;
To be loved as to love.

For it is in giving that we receive;
It is in pardoning that we are pardoned;
And it is in dying that we are born to eternal life. Amen.

(National Shrine of St. Francis of Assisi, www.shrinesf.org/franciscan -prayer.html)

For Reflection and Discussion:

View a video clip of Archbishop Gregory Aymond of New Orleans as he speaks about life issues in our day and the teachings of Jesus. The clip can be found on the CMN website at http://catholicsmobilizing.org/reading-guide/. Discuss Archbishop Aymond's perspective on capital punishment as one of several issues in an ethics of life.

Key Points of Chapter 3

- Jesus teaches us to forgo retaliation and to love our enemies.

- Nonretaliation is not passive. In the Sermon on the Mount, Jesus teaches us to act in a way that faces up to injustice and responds with goodness.

- Loving our enemies means wanting and working for their good. Loving our enemies is consistent with justice. In the context of convicted murderers, it means working for a prison sentence that matches the gravity of the crime and the moral status of the offender.

- "Moral status," here, means whether the offender is an adult who knowingly and willfully kills another, whether the offender is in his or her youth and still in a period of maturation, whether the person is mentally ill or disabled, and so on. The offender's moral status matters because one goal of imprisonment is to provide opportunity for the person to recognize his or her sins and crimes and to turn his or her life around.

- Punishment does not have the purpose of making a person worse or to experience inhumane conditions of life. Punishment should leave open the possibility that the offender will heal and start to strive for the good and to be a better person.

- However, we cannot depend upon the reform of a murderer. Jesus' teachings on nonretaliation and love of enemies fulfill the law by indicating how victims can act in accord with the justice and mercy of God. By doing good, victims and victims' families can experience some healing.

4

The New Evangelization

Pope John Paul II often repeated his call for a "new evangelization." He did so while visiting the United States in 1999. The new evangelization includes a call to be "unconditionally pro-life," to "proclaim, celebrate and serve the Gospel of life in every situation," and to join together "to end the death penalty."[1] For John Paul II, the new evangelization is not new inasmuch as it is a proclamation of salvation and reconciliation with God in Jesus Christ. It is not entirely new in its emphasis on the role of laypeople in evangelization amid their day-to-day lives. This role of the laity is an important theme of Vatican II (1962–65). However, the new evangelization does have a new emphasis on the transformation of culture and the social teachings of the church. John Paul II envisions that we will live out our "culture of life" in all aspects of social life and that this culture of life will have an evangelical role in the transformation of society. Through the culture of life, we will evangelize secular cultures, which— these days—are tempted to slide toward a culture of death.

Catholic opposition to the death penalty does not begin (or end) with the papacy of John Paul II. However, he does provide theoretical clarity, and he emphasizes the practical importance of opposition to capital punishment. "Theoretical clarity" means that John Paul spells out the purposes, proper goals, and appropriate uses of the death penalty. In theory, he notes that a recourse to the execution of violent criminals is possible in terms of self-defense. The death penalty is justifiable if there is no other means to protect society. To this degree, he also indicates that such cases will be "very rare, if not practically non-existent."[2] On the practical level, he holds that Catholic opposition to the death penalty is a sign of faith and hope.

Sr. Helen Prejean

"The living tradition of the church is always emerging out of the dialogue we Catholics engage in head-on with the suffering world. . . .

I found myself saying to the Holy Father: 'Walking with this man to his death, the essence of the Gospel of Jesus becomes very clear: what are you for? compassion or vengeance? love or hate? life or death?' There's nothing like seeing the reality of state killing close-up to clarify what we really believe" ("Foreword," *Where Justice and Mercy Meet: Catholic Opposition to the Death Penalty* [Collegeville, MN: Liturgical Press, 2013], xii–xiii).

In a world where people are often used by others and life is cheap, opposition to the death penalty is "a sign of hope . . . that the dignity of human life must never be taken away."[3] Opposition to capital punishment is part of the whole cloth of pro-life evangelization—of opposition to abortion, euthanasia, the exploitation of the vulnerable, as well as the militarization of cultures, genocide, and other war crimes.[4] On one level, the death penalty is conceivable if a government has no other way to protect its citizens. On another, more practical level, opposition to the death penalty is part of a renewed way of bringing Christ to the world.

The Protection and Good of Society

The death penalty has its logic in the principles of self-defense. In the words of the *Catechism of the Catholic Church*, "Someone who defends his life is not guilty of murder even if he is forced to deal his aggressor a lethal blow."[5] As the *Catechism* develops this moral principle further, it clarifies the point by noting when the use of force goes too far. On this point, the *Catechism* cites St. Thomas Aquinas: "If a man in self-defense uses more than necessary violence, it will be unlawful: whereas if he repels force with moderation, his defense will be lawful."[6] In defending ourselves, we ought not to intend to kill. We ought to intend to protect and save innocent lives, including our own. Clearly, the intention to protect the innocent outweighs a concern for the life of an aggressor. Violence involved in protection against an aggressor is, in a moral sense, actually directed toward the protection of the aggressor's victims. The moral aim concerns the innocent, and the violence against the aggressor is, in a moral sense, indirect.

This logic of self-defense is the framework for understanding the death penalty. It is an act of self-defense—when a government seeks to protect its citizens from someone who cannot be constrained by other means. If we consider that the preservation and good of society is the logic behind both punishment and the death penalty, we have reason to oppose capital punishment as part of the current system of punishment.

To this degree, the placement of the death penalty within self-defense is significant. In effect, "capital" punishment is taken out of punishment and placed within protection. The *Catechism of the Catholic Church* separates the possibility of recourse to the death penalty from an outline of punishment and its purposes. Punishment can be put to a variety of purposes. It has the purpose of a deterrent to "curb" harmful behavior—like double fines when speeding or running a stop sign in a school zone. It has the purpose of "redressing the disorder" caused by the offense and of "inflict[ing] punishment proportionate to the gravity of the offense" (2266).

This purpose of addressing the crime and redressing disorder has a retributive element. We impose a measure of punishment upon the criminal as payback. This kind of "payback" is not revenge or vengeance. It is not intended to hurt or destroy the offender but to begin to turn his or her life around. If the guilty person accepts the payback willingly, he or she is set right in relationship to society. The offender "pays a debt to society," as the saying goes. If accepted willingly and with an attitude of repentance, punishment can be medicinal. It can be healing and reconciling. In short, punishment has a whole set of purposes. The *Catechism*, however, does not apply these various reasons for punishment to the death penalty. In the *Catechism*, the death penalty is not located among the explanations for punishment.

When the *Catechism* deals with the death penalty, it returns to the more precise logic of self-defense. "[T]he traditional teaching of the Church does not exclude recourse to the death penalty, if this is the only possible way of effectively defending human lives against the unjust aggressor" (2267). Punishment—redressing disorder, for example—certainly includes the purpose of defending society. But the inverse is not the case. Self-defense does not necessarily include punishment. The *Catechism* does not include the death penalty in deliberations about punishment. For example, it is not included in determinations about "punishment proportionate to the gravity of the offense" (2266).

Notice how closely the following statement from the *Catechism* conforms to the logic of self-defense:

> If, however, non-lethal means are sufficient to defend and protect people's safety from the aggressor, authority will limit itself to such means, as these are more in keeping with the concrete conditions of the common good and more in conformity with the dignity of the human person. (2267)

Further, the *Catechism* cites John Paul II's *Evangelium Vitae* (56), which turns from a theory or philosophical consideration to practical realities. Situations where execution, as self-defense, is needed "are very rare, if not practically non-existent" because we have other means of "rendering one who has committed an offense incapable of doing harm" (*Catechism* 2267).

John Paul II holds that, in our day, the use of the death penalty —if not used very rarely—actually contributes to a disorder in society, a disorder that tends to disregard the full dignity of human life. Opposition to the death penalty is a sign of our commitment to human dignity and to life.

> If such great care must be taken to respect every life, even that of criminals and unjust aggressors, the commandment "You shall not kill" has absolute value when it refers to the innocent person. And all the more so in the case of weak and defenseless human beings, who find their ultimate defense against the arrogance and caprice of others only in the absolute binding force of God's commandment. (*Evangelium Vitae* 57)

We have seen this logic before. It is the logic of the Bible. Taking the life of another is such a grave offense that refusing to take the life of a murderer shows, all the more, the dignity and inestimable worth of human life.

Arbitrariness

"The studies consistently show that those who kill white victims are much more likely to receive the death penalty than those who kill black victims."

"Racial disparities in sentencing and executions suggest that race plays a role in the application of the death penalty."

"States vary enormously in the quality of representation they provide to indigent defendants. . . . The *National Law Journal* . . . concluded that capital trials are 'more like a random flip of the coin' . . . because the [court appointed] defense attorney is 'too often . . . ill-trained, unprepared [and] grossly underpaid.'"

(Death Penalty Information Center, www.deathpenaltyinfo.org /arbitrariness)

In addition, this Catholic concern for the dignity of life and opposition to the death penalty gives special emphasis to how the poor and marginalized are disproportionately imprisoned and executed in the United States. The practical use of the death penalty has had a disproportionate effect on minorities and the poor. As disproportionate, the use of the death penalty has been unjust. Today and throughout its history in the United States, the death penalty has not played a role in restoring order. Rather it has perpetuated social injustices and injustices within the legal system. As one experienced lawyer has put it, "If you're going to commit murder, you want to be white, and you want to be wealthy—so that you can hire a first-class lawyer—and you want to kill a black person. And if [you are], the odds of your being sentenced to death are basically zero."[7] The inverse is also the case. The evidence is clear that the severity of the crime is not a key factor in the implementation of the death penalty. Instead the key factors are more arbitrary:

- the state where the crime is committed (most executions are in the South),

- the race of offender and victim,

- reliance on a public defender,

- and gender.[8]

If justice is our concern, capital punishment is part of the problem.

For Reflection and Discussion:

Bryan Stevenson is the executive director of the Equal Justice Initiative (www.eji.org). He and the EJI advocate and defend the poor and minorities in the justice system, where bias against them is well documented. In the video provided at http://catholics mobilizing.org/reading-guide/, Bryan tells the story of his life and work and offers information about injustices in our court system. After listening to his story, reflect on how the death penalty perpetuates injustices in our system of criminal justice.

The Catholic Tradition

Many who have been raised in the church have learned that the use of the death penalty is permissible. They have learned that an acceptance of capital punishment imposed by the state has been part of the Catholic tradition. Sometimes, this "permissibility" and "acceptance" have been taught as "responsibility" and "obligation." In other words, the Catholic Church has allowed the state the moral right to impose death as a penalty for some crimes, but some of us have been taught that the state has the "responsibility" and "obligation" to impose the death penalty. This view is incorrect. To state the church's historical view in this way is far too simplistic. "Permissibility" is far from "required." The confusion is understandable. In centuries past, the death penalty was seen as a sign that taking another person's life is intolerable. Today, the church's pro-life stance communicates the same concern. But it has taken on a more consistent form: refusing to impose death has become a sign of the dignity and inestimable value of all human life.

Church History and Tradition

Throughout its history, the church's stance on the death penalty has been woven together with issues related to church and state. The death penalty has never been a policy of the church *per se*. Because it is a prerogative of the state, the church's stance on the death penalty has been intertwined with the complexities and developments of the relationship between the church and worldly empires and governments. Amid these developments, it may be helpful to note that John Paul II's call for the practical abolition of the death penalty is in line with developments of the church's spiritual authority in the modern era (especially since the late nineteenth century). As the church has become less tied to secular authorities, its view of the death penalty has become less complicated. A simple "no" becomes more thinkable.

A "no" to the death penalty is hardly "simple," but today it is nearly definitive. We have seen that the *Catechism of the Catholic Church* cites John Paul II's phrase that the death penalty ought to be "very rare, if not practically non-existent" (2267; *Evangelium Vitae* 56). If the history of the death penalty is complex, justifications for it and theories about it are equally diverse and overlapping. In 1976, the Vatican offered guidance to the United States bishops on the matter of the death penalty and the history of the church. Rather than survey two thousand years of church history, consider this statement offered by the Pontifical Commission for Justice and Peace: "The church has never directly addressed the question of the state's right to exercise the death penalty."[9] The emphasis of this claim is on the word "directly." The church had indirectly supported the death penalty as a right of the state. But not until recently has it directly considered capital punishment in terms of the church's faith and its mission.

The Vatican instruction of 1976 outlines various theoretical justifications for capital punishment and notes that none of them seem to hold in practice. The tradition holds that punishment ought to be medicinal. But capital punishment "negates the possibility of the criminal to rehabilitate himself." The tradition carries forward the purpose of retribution—that a criminal should be punished in a way that reestablishes order and metes out a punishment as "payback" for the crime. But the Pontifical Commission holds that "*serious questions* can be raised on humanitarian grounds for the state to practice a merely vindictive type of penalty." The tradition holds out the possibility that the death penalty might provide an example to others. But, according to the Commission, there is no conclusive evidence of "any meaningful correlation between the death penalty and the ratio of serious criminality." Further, the reality of capital punishment is "that it is practiced unfairly by being used more against the poor and the marginalized in society."[10]

Finally, the Pontifical Commission points to an "inner logic" of the church's stance on the sacredness of life, including opposition to abortion and euthanasia. The Commission calls Catholics "to be consistent in this defense and extend it to the practices of capital punishment." In short, the Vatican Commission holds that "for the ethical values involved and because of the lack of probative arguments to the contrary, the abolition of capital punishment is to be favored."[11]

We have seen that the *Catechism of the Catholic Church* (1997) provides clarity and develops the Commission's perspective. It does so by drawing on the teachings of John Paul II's *Evangelium Vitae* and its focus on self-defense. The *Catechism* upholds the tradition by pointing to a continuous thread in the tradition (self-defense). By pointing to self-defense, it allows the other threads—like capital punishment as retribution or deterrence—to unravel. In short, the death penalty is maintained in theory as self-defense, rather than punishment. As self-defense, it remains a prospect only in theory as long as secure imprisonment is a possibility. In societies with systems of incarceration, a pastoral and practical disavowal of the death penalty becomes part of the church's evangelization of the world and its pro-life mission. In effect, the sacredness of life is the principle that allows the death penalty in theory (as self-defense) but calls us to work against it in practice.

Free Will, Responsibility, and Deterrence

The Catholic moral tradition emphasizes human free will and our responsibility for our actions. Many support capital punishment precisely for this reason. For some, holding to the death penalty underlines the fact that we respect free will and that people are in control of what they do and who they become. Sometimes it appears that those who are against the death penalty want to blame society and social conditions for a person's crime. Sometimes it appears that "cycles of violence" in society are blamed, as if the criminal "didn't know any better." In the face of this lack of accountability, the death penalty seems to be a way to assert that we have free will and responsibility for who we are and what we do.

This call for moral responsibility fits with thinking about the death penalty as a deterrent. According to the logic of deterrence, if a person is responsible for his or her actions and if the death penalty is in place, then a murderer has final responsibility for the punishment of death. In a sense, he or she has chosen it. However, the reality of deterrence is not this simple. The deterrent effect of the death penalty has been studied for over three decades, and the results are inconclusive. States that institute capital punishment do not see a decline in the murder rate. In most states, murder rates and execution rates rise together. In any case, there is no clear evidence on the death penalty as a deterrent.[12] Consider this: "The consensus among criminologists is that the death penalty does not add any significant deterrent effect above that of long-term imprisonment."[13]

Deterrence

"The vast majority of the world's top criminologists believe that the empirical research has revealed the deterrence hypothesis for a myth. . . . Recent econometric studies, which posit that the death penalty has a marginal deterrent effect beyond that of long-term imprisonment, are so limited or flawed that they have failed to undermine consensus.

In short, the consensus among criminologists is that the death penalty does not add any significant deterrent effect above that of long-term imprisonment" (Michael L. Radelet and Traci L. Lacock, "Do Executions Lower Homicide Rates?," *The Journal of Criminal Law and Criminology* 99:2 [2009]).

The important point for us is this: a call for responsibility does not depend on the death penalty. In fact, the movement for restorative justice is opposed to capital punishment precisely because it expects offenders to take responsibility for their actions. It is imaginable, certainly, that life in prison will provide time for a murderer to realize and accept his or her responsibility. Accepting responsibility is key to rehabilitation and conversion. And rehabilitation—insofar as it requires personal responsibility—does not mean that a person is free from punishment. Rehabilitation means that a person accepts his or her punishment as just. For this reason, a call for responsibility and a defense of free will are achieved through lengthy prison sentences.[14] A disavowal of the death penalty is fully consistent with a call to responsibility.

Before we leave the topic of deterrence, we should repeat the significance of the church's teaching on the death penalty in relationship to self-defense. Even if capital punishment were effective as a deterrent, it would not be justifiable on that basis. In *Responsibility, Rehabilitation, and Restoration*, the US bishops state,

> [R]egardless of their impact, not all methods of reducing crime are consistent with the teachings of the Church and the ideals of our nation. For example, even if the death penalty were proven to be a deterrent to crime, the Catholic bishops would still oppose its use because there are alternative means to protect society available to us today.[15]

For Reflection and Discussion:

In a speech to a legal association (October 2014), Pope Francis called "Christians and all people of good will" to work, not only against the death penalty and inhumane conditions in prisons but also against life in prison, which he called a "hidden" sentence of death.[16] The pope's call might be considered controversial, as many people think of life in prison without parole as placement for the death penalty. The pope's call, however, is consistent with the traditional purposes of punishment. Reflect on this issue.

Also consider a related issue. Today, "approximately 2,500 individuals are serving a life sentence without possibility of parole for crimes committed as children." Juveniles serving life without parole (JLWOP) are unique to the United States.[17] The Supreme Court has ruled against the death penalty and mandatory JLWOP, but the sentence is still used in several states. Is JLWOP a hidden sentence of death for a young person?

Closure for Victims' Families

Some claim that the death penalty is needed in order to provide closure for family members of victims. Many family members of victims state the contrary, that life in prison is a much better solution. Some go further and claim that imposing the death penalty would show disrespect for the memory of their murdered loved one. Some say one thing; others say the opposite. It is not possible to settle the debate on whether or not the death penalty should be expected to provide satisfaction and closure for victims' families. Their expectations, hopes, and desires will differ. However, we—people of faith—do have reasons and responsibilities to listen to those who want the memories of murdered family members to be a sign of faith and hope.

O Mary . . .

Grant that all who believe in your Son
may proclaim the Gospel of life
with honesty and love
to the people of our time.

Obtain for them the grace
to accept that Gospel
as a gift ever new,
the joy of celebrating it with gratitude
throughout their lives
and the courage to bear witness to it
resolutely, in order to build,
together with all people of good will,
the civilization of truth and love,
to the praise and glory of God,
the Creator and lover of life.

(John Paul II, *Evangelium Vitae* 105)

Consider the stories and statements of members of Journey of Hope at www.journeyofhope.org. It is an organization founded by family members of murder victims. These family members "call for alternatives to the death penalty and an end to the cycle of violence that capital punishment perpetuates in our society." The organization "stresses the need for offender accountability and the opportunity for the offender to make things right with the victim as much as possible." They believe that this kind of restorative justice "allow[s] for greater healing in the lives of victims and offenders, and peace in communities, after crimes are committed" (www.journeyofhope.org/who-we-are/).

Consider the words of Marietta Jaeger-Lane, whose seven-year-old daughter Susie was kidnapped and murdered:

> Loved ones, wrenched from our lives by violent crime, deserve more beautiful, noble and honorable memorials than premeditated, state-sanctioned killings. The death penalty only creates more victims and more grieving families. By becoming that which we deplore—people who kill people—we insult the sacred memory of all our precious victims.[18]

Consider the life story of Bill Pelke, who suggests that forgiveness might be the best pathway to closure—if closure is at all possible. Bill's grandmother, Ruth Elizabeth Pelke, was murdered by a group of teenagers, led presumably by fourteen-year-old Paula Cooper. In Bill's book *Journey of Hope*, he recounts his spiritual transformation. After the death of his grandmother, Nana, his life spiraled downward in depression and despair. Through the memory of Nana's love and faith, he prayed for the ability to forgive. He experienced conversion and personal transformation. About healing and closure he says this:

> It is difficult to deal with the pain and some never heal. That is why many of the victims' families on the Journey [the organization, Journey of Hope] promote forgiveness as a way of healing. It was how they healed. But forgiveness is so misunderstood. Many think that to forgive the bad guy is doing him a favor. The person who forgives is the one who gets the favor.
>
> On many occasions, I have told people that forgiving Paula Cooper did more for me than it did for Paula Cooper. That's the way forgiveness is.[19]

For Reflection and Discussion:

View a talk given by Marietta Jaeger-Lane as she discusses her struggles with forgiveness and hope. It can be found on the CMN website at http://catholicsmobilizing.org/reading-guide/. Reflect on her claim that capital punishment "desperately disappoints the families [of murder victims] and degrades, dehumanizes, and debilitates us as a society."

Key Points of Chapter 4

- In the Catholic moral tradition, killing ought never to be one's direct or primary intention. Killing another person is permissible as self-defense. It is foreseen as a possible outcome of protecting life. But killing is not an outcome that is sought for its own sake.

- The reasons provided by the church for the use of the death penalty pertain to self-defense. According to the *Catechism*, execution is not an option as a direct means of punishment.

- In practical terms, the death penalty does not provide a means to achieve the traditional goals of punishment. These goals are redressing a crime, restoring order in society, providing a deterrent, and sustaining the possibility for the rehabilitation of the offender.

- Opposition to the death penalty corresponds to a call for a more just society. In practical terms, the implementation of the death penalty has unjustly targeted the poor. It has also suffered from racial bias.

- Opposition to the death penalty has become part of the church's pro-life stance and the new evangelization.

- The current teachings of the church on the death penalty represent a change, but this change is not a radical break. The current position of the church has continuity within its history and tradition. The continuity is found in the church's faith in Christ and principles about human dignity.

- Many family members of murder victims hope that the memories of their murdered loved ones will be signs of faith and hope. They want no part in capital punishment. On the contrary, they see the possibility of a life-giving response to murder. That life-giving response animates their opposition to the death penalty.

Notes

Preface

1. United States Conference of Catholic Bishops (USCCB), "A Culture of Life and the Penalty of Death" (Washington, DC: USCCB, 2005), www.usccb.org/issues-and-action/human-life-and-dignity/death -penalty-capital-punishment/upload/penaltyofdeath.pdf.

2. USCCB, "Restorative Justice: Healing and Transformation of Persons, Families and Communities" (Washington, DC: USCCB, 2015), www.usccb.org/issues-and-action/human-life-and-dignity/criminal -justice-restorative-justice/upload/Restorative-Justice-Backgrounder -2015-02.pdf.

3. Tim Carpenter, "Clergy Plead for the Repeal of Kansas Death Penalty," *The Topeka Capital-Journal, CJonline.com* (February 10, 2015), cjonline.com/news/state/2015-02-10/clergy-plead-repeal-kansas -death-penalty.

Chapter 1: God Is the Giver of Life

1. Pope Francis, *Evangelii Gaudium* (Libreria Editrice Vaticana, November 24, 2013), 24.

2. The despair of the exiles is powerfully expressed in Psalm 137.

3. USCCB, "Bishops' Statement on Capital Punishment, 1980," www .usccb.org/issues-and-action/human-life-and-dignity/death-penalty -capital-punishment/statement-on-capital-punishment.cfm.

Chapter 2: Restorative Justice

1. Brian Haas, "Tennessee's death penalty is back on track," *The Tennessean* (October 23, 2013), archive.tennessean.com/article/20131023 /NEWS21/112040002/10-23-2013-Tennessee-s-death-penalty-back-track.

2. Gary Strauss, "Ohio Killer's Slow Execution Raises Controversy," *USA Today* (January 16, 2014), www.usatoday.com/story/news/nation/2014/01/16/ohio-killer-executed-with-new-lethal-drug-combo/4512651/.

3. "Letter to the editor: 'Eye for an eye' is just punishment," *The Tennessean* (February 13, 2014), www.tennessean.com/story/news/local/gallatin/opinion/2014/02/14/letter-to-the-editor-eye-for-an-eye-is-just-punishment/5462745/.

4. What Jews call the Torah, Christians call the Pentateuch (referring to the five books).

5. The *lex talionis* is part of the Hammurabi Code, which dates back to about 1700 BC or to the time of Israel's patriarchs (e.g., Jacob). The exodus from Egypt occurs at about 1300 BC.

6. *The Catholic Study Bible*, ed. Donald Senior, John J. Collins, and Mary Ann Getty (New York: Oxford University Press, 2011), 108.

7. Ibid., 166.

8. Ibid., 1344.

9. Richard Buck, "Biblical Principles: Mosaic Law," in *Where Justice and Mercy Meet: Catholic Opposition to the Death Penalty*, ed. Vicki Schieber, Trudy D. Conway, and David Matzko McCarthy, 88 (Collegeville, MN: Liturgical Press, 2013). The question is attributed to Rabbi Shimon Bar Yochai, who was active in the first and second centuries CE.

10. Ibid., 90.

11. Ibid., 93.

12. Ibid., 92.

13. One example of this out-of-context use is by Fordham University law professor Thane Rosenbaum, in his *Payback: The Case for Revenge* (Chicago: University of Chicago Press, 2013). Rosenbaum repeatedly appeals to the biblical "an eye for an eye" as a command for revenge without ever putting the phrase in its biblical context.

Chapter 3: Responding to Evil with Good

1. "The hands of the witnesses shall be the first raised to put the person to death, and afterward the hands of all the people. Thus shall you purge the evil from your midst" (Deut 17:7).

2. Consider the requirements of Deuteronomy 19:15-21: "One witness alone shall not stand against someone in regard to any crime or any offense that may have been committed; a charge shall stand only on the testimony of two or three witnesses. If a hostile witness rises against someone to accuse that person of wrongdoing, the two parties in the dispute shall appear in the presence of the LORD, in the presence of the priests and judges in office at that time, and the judges must investigate

it thoroughly. If the witness is a false witness and has falsely accused the other, you shall do to the false witness just as that false witness planned to do to the other. Thus shall you purge the evil from your midst. The rest shall hear and be afraid, and never again do such an evil thing as this in your midst. Do not show pity. Life for life, eye for eye, tooth for tooth, hand for hand, and foot for foot!"

3. Brian Rogers, "Texas Sets Man Free from Death Row," *Houston Chronicle*, October 27, 2010, www.chron.com/news/houston-texas /article/Texas-sets-man-free-from-death-row-1619337.php.

4. Sr. Mary Katherine Birge, "WWJD? Jesus, the Death Penalty, and US Catholics," in *Where Justice and Mercy Meet: Catholic Opposition to the Death Penalty*, ed. Vicki Schieber, Trudy D. Conway, and David Matzko McCarthy, 100n8 (Collegeville, MN: Liturgical Press, 2013).

5. N. T. Wright, *Matthew for Everyone*, Part I (Louisville: Westminster John Knox, 2004), 52.

6. Antoinette Bosco is an author of several books and has her own website: www.antoinettebosco.com.

7. "Forgiveness and Healing," in *Where Justice and Mercy Meet*, 59–61, 67–68.

8. "What is Reconciliation?," Murder Victims' Families for Reconciliation, www.mvfr.org/about/what-is-reconciliation.

9. "The Death Penalty: How It Causes Harm," Murder Victims' Families for Reconciliation, www.mvfr.org/death-penalty (used with permission).

Chapter 4: The New Evangelization

1. John Paul II, Homily (St. Louis: January 27, 1999), w2.vatican.va /content/john-paul-ii/en/travels/1999/documents/hf_jp-ii_hom _27011999_stlouis.html.

2. John Paul II, *Evangelium Vitae* (Rome: Libreria Editrice Vaticana, 1995), 56.

3. John Paul II, Homily (St. Louis: January 27, 1999).

4. John Paul II, *Urbi et Orbi* Message (December 25, 1998), www .vatican.va/holy_father/john_paul_ii/messages/urbi/documents/hf _jp-ii_mes_25121998_urbi_en.html.

5. *Catechism of the Catholic Church*, 2nd ed. (United States Catholic Conference—Libreria Editrice Vaticana, 1997), 2264.

6. Thomas Aquinas, *Summa Theologiae* II–II, q. 64, a. 7.

7. Laura Fitzpatrick, "The Death Penalty: Racist, Classist, and Unfair," *Time* (February 23, 2010), content.time.com/time/nation/article /0,8599,1967233,00.html.

8. See "Arbitrariness," Death Penalty Information Center, www.death penaltyinfo.org/arbitrariness.

9. Pontifical Commission for Justice and Peace, "The Church and the Death Penalty," *Origins* 6, no. 25 (December 9, 1976): 391.

10. Ibid.

11. Ibid.

12. Jongmook Choe, "Another Look at the Deterrent Effect of Death Penalty," *Journal of Advanced Research in Law and Economics* (Summer 2010). Aaron Chalfin, Amelia M. Haviland, and Steven Raphael, "What Do Panel Studies Tell Us About a Deterrent Effect of Capital Punishment?," *Journal of Quantitative Criminology* (2013).

13. Michael L. Radelet and Traci L. Lacock, "Do Executions Lower Homicide Rates?: The Views of Leading Criminologists," *The Journal of Criminal Law and Criminology* 99, no. 2 (2009): 489–508, at 504.

14. It should be noted that children who commit murder are in a different moral situation in relationship to the full knowledge and freedom of their acts. The mentally disabled are in a different situation as well.

15. USCCB, *Responsibility, Rehabilitation, and Restoration: A Catholic Perspective on Crime and Criminal Justice* (November 15, 2000), www.usccb.org/issues-and-action/human-life-and-dignity/criminal-justice-restorative-justice/crime-and-criminal-justice.cfm.

16. Address of Pope Francis to the Delegates of the International Association of Penal Law (October 23, 2014), m.vatican.va/content/francesco/en/speeches/2014/october/documents/papa-francesco_20141023_associazione-internazionale-diritto-penale.html.

17. Joshua Rovner, The Sentencing Project, "Juvenile Life Without Parole: An Overview," sentencingproject.org/doc/publications/jj_Juvenile_Life_Without_Parole.pdf.

18. "Marietta Jaeger-Lane," www.journeyofhope.org/who-we-are/murder-victim-family/marietta-jaeger-lane/.

19. Ines Aubert, "Interview with Bill Pelke, founder of the Journey of Hope" (February 2007), lifespark.org/download/reports-interviews/PelkeInterview.pdf.